MARY,
FRIED CANARY

Laurence Anholt wrote the rhymes,
Arthur Robins drew the lines.

ORCHARD BOOKS

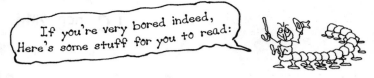

If you're very bored indeed, Here's some stuff for you to read:

This magnificent little book was published by those CHARMING people at

ORCHARD BOOKS

who all live together at:

338 Euston Road, London NW1 3BH

(You can send them a Christmas card if you like.)

Published down under by

Level 17/207 Kent Street, Sydney, NSW 2000

Hachette Children's Books

Orchard Books Australia

First published in Great Britain in 2002. First paperback edition 2003

Blah, blah, blahdy blah...

Dooby dooby dooby doo..

A CIP catalogue record for this book is available from the British Library.

etc, etc...

Does anyone read this stuff?

ISBN 978 1 84121 010 0 (hardback)

ISBN 978 1 84121 018 6 (paperback)

1 3 5 7 9 10 8 6 4 2 (hardback)

5 7 9 10 8 6 4 (paperback)

ARE YOU STILL THERE?

Printed in Great Britain

Goodnight.

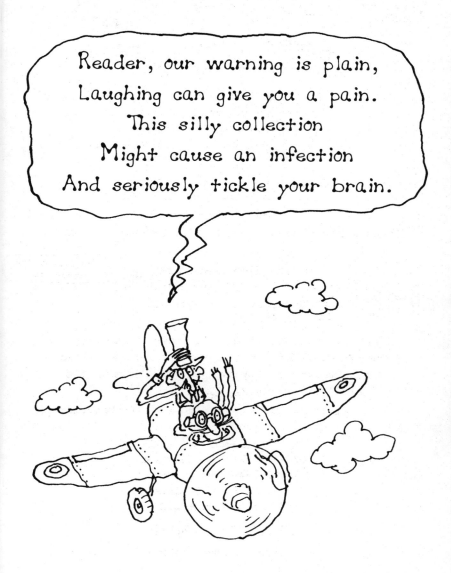

SPOT ALL THE SERIOUSLY SILLY PEOPLE!

Old King Cole ☆ Doctor Foster ☆ Cool Queen Wenceslas
Humpty Dumpty ☆ Bendy Burglar ☆ Incey Wincey ☆ Silly Sand Man

Really Frilly

YUM!

Sam the Man ☆ Johnny Stout ☆ Little Bo-Peep ☆ The Queen
Mary, Mary ☆ The Deadly Dinner Ladies ☆ Greedy Green Martian

CONTENTS

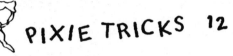

NUTTY NURSERY CRIME

I am a little nut tree,
Nothing will I wear,
But some frilly underpants
Tied around my hair.

The King of Spain's daughter
Came to visit me.
She said I was as loopy
As a hairy chimpanzee.

She said, "You'll go to prison
For all these nutty crimes.
I reckon you've been reading
Those *Seriously Silly Rhymes.*"

SCARY MARY

Mary, Mary, fried canary,
How does your garden grow?
With plastic gnomes in plastic homes
All fishing in a row.

Mary, Mary, slightly hairy,
In a big steamroller,
Chasing bees and squashing trees
And drinking cans of cola.

PIXIE TRICKS

My mother said I never should
Play with the pixies in the wood.

If I did, she would warn,
You'll turn into a giant prawn.

Your tail will curl, you'll turn bright pink,
We'll have to keep you in the sink.

A naughty girl is what you are,
I'll put you in a pickle jar.

HIS HAIRY HIGHNESS

Oh, the grand old duke of York,
He had ten thousand hairs.

He combed them up on the top of his head

And he combed them down again.

When they were up, he was tall.

When they were down, he was small.

When they were only halfway up,
Then he couldn't see at all.

POTTY-POODLE-DOODLE

Doctor Foster went to Gloucester
In a high-speed train.

He tripped on a poodle
Which ate his Pot Noodle,

So he flew home on a plane.

SMELLY SHOE SONG

There was an old woman who lived
    in a shoe.
I wouldn't like it, neither would you.
    Her children said, "Mummy,
    Our house is quite crummy
And smelly as pelican poo."

PRICKLY POEM

Georgie Porgie, pudding and pie,
Kissed the girls and made them cry.
The idea of a snog was fine
But Georgie was a porcupine.

He's been eating prickled onions too!

A PILE OF POETRY

A tiny young writer from Gower
Found poetry gave him great power.
Although he was small,
His poems were tall,
And he stacked up his words like a

    T
      O
      W
        E
        R.

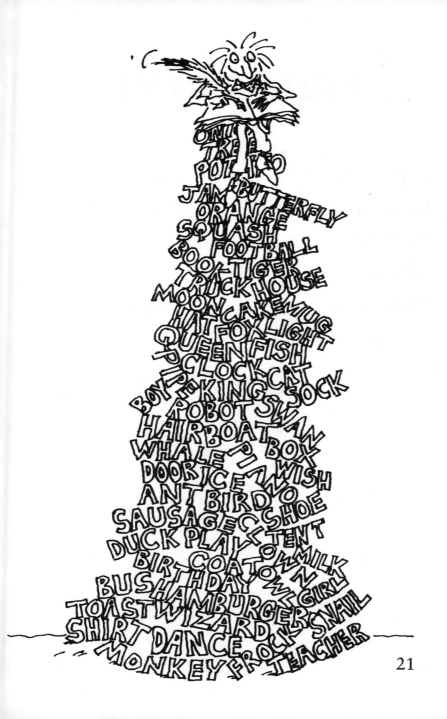

21

OLD MOTHER'S MOBILE

Old Mother Hubbard
Went to the cupboard
To give her poor doggy a bone.
The dog said,

Ring, ring!
You silly old thing,
That bone was a
mobile phone.

She went to the park
To throw him a ball.
Her dog said,

Hang on,
I'm taking a call.

She went to the doctor
To take out the phone.
The doctor just muttered,

I don't like his tone.

She said to the dog,
"Enough of your tricks."
The doggy just answered,

It's cheap after six.

She said to the dog,
"What will you do next?"
The doggy replied,
"Just send me a text."

She went to the vet.
The dog was outraged.
"Will you be quiet,
I'm already engaged."

Mother Hubbard was crying,
"What else can we do?"
Her doggy said,

E-mails.
Computer games, too.

SHELL SHOCK

Humpty Dumpty fell on his shell,
Humpty Dumpty feeling unwell.
All the king's soldiers also felt shaken
About scrambled eggs without any
bacon.

This poem was made using a free-range egg.

HIDE-AND-SEEK FEET

Little Bo Peep has lost her feet
And doesn't know where to find them.
Look in your shoe, you'll find one
    or two,
And those are your toes beside them.

COOL CAT RAP

Pussy cat, pussy cat,
Where have you been?

Pussy cat, pussy cat,
What did you do?

Pussy cat, pussy cat,
What did you buy?

Pussy cat, pussy cat,
You really look nice.

Pussy cat, pussy cat,
What else did you do?
"The queen bought a crop-top
To match her tattoo."

Pussy cat, pussy cat,
Why are you yawning?

We danced at
a nightclub
Till early next
morning.

WEENY WEDDING

Solomon Grundy,
Born on Monday,

Christened on Tuesday,

Married on Wednesday.

His wife said, "Maybe
I've married a baby.
I've been told
he's three days old."

RAINING CATS AND DOGS

It's
r
a
i
n
i
n
g

It's
p
o
u
r
i
n
g

The maths class is boring.
We stayed in bed to sleep instead,
So half the class is snoring.

YANKEE HANKY-PANKY

Yankee Doodle went to town
Riding on a broomstick.
A woolly yak sat on his back
And made him feel quite seasick.

COOL QUEEN WENCESLAS

Good Queen Wenceslas looked out,
On the Feast of Michael,
When a poor man came in sight,
Riding on a cycle.

Brightly shone the poor man's nose
'Cos the frost was cruel.
(Several snowmen stood in rows
Looking kind of co-o-ol.)

"Yo, you dude, you're really poor
And your beard is crusty.
Please don't hang around my door
Your bike is awfully rusty."

Ma'am, those words are
    harsh and chill
And really not that funny.
I am older than the hills,
With very little money.

Good Queen Wenceslas felt bad
For being quite so stingy.
"I will help this poor old lad
Although he is quite whingey.

Come in and have a bath, old mate.
(You're really rather smelly.)
Here's a sandwich on a plate,
Relax and watch the telly.

I'm sorry, pal, for seeming hard
And being sort of iffy.
I'll just grab my credit card.
I'll be back in a jiffy."

Then Queen Wenceslas went down
And did a ton of shopping,
Went to every store in town,
Hardly even stopping.

At last the homeward road she took
To her humble castle.

Hello Grandad, come and look
At your lovely parcels.

"I have bought you food and stuff
And this nifty scooter.
Boy, I really spent enough
On your new computer."

Then the old boy did appear
Looking quite amazing.
He was dressed in trendy gear,
He'd even done some shaving.

"Blimey!" thought the goodly Queen.

This fella's really funky.
His hair is neat, his teeth are clean.
I'd say he's pretty hunky.

And so the Queen let out a sigh,
She saw what she'd been missing.
She grabbed the poor man by his tie
And soon they started kissing.

The moral of this lovely song:
(In case you're not too clever)
First impressions can be wrong
But true love lasts for e-e-ver.

CROCO-SMILE

There was a young dentist named
    Kylie,
Whose patients all thought of her
    highly.
    One affectionate soul
    Swallowed her whole,
Then reclined in the chair looking
    smiley.

WIDDLY PIDDLY POEM

Hey diddle diddle,
A whale did a widdle
All over the classroom floor.
The giraffe just laughed
To see such fun,
And the boar did a little bit more.

ALL ABOUT
THE AUTHOR

When Laurence was a little lad
His weeknus wuz his spelig.
Wel, iz yor speeling beter now?
But Laurence is knot telig.

He tried his hand at this and that,
At last, became a writer.
He finds it best to work in bed.
(The lazy little blighter.)

He has a decent set of teeth,
One strangely twisted toe.
He's written nearly eighty books,
That's all you need to know.

ALL ABOUT
THE ILLUSTRATOR

When Arthur was a new-born babe
The doctors stared in awe.
As Arthur grabbed a pencil,
And the child began to draw.

Wow, that kiddy sure was good,
He's still drawing now.
He could draw an octopus
Riding on a cow.

So go and buy his lovely books,
You never will be bored.
And you will see exactly why
He won that Gold Award*.

* Smarties Gold Award

47

SERIOUSLY SILLY RHYMES and STORIES

Laurence Anholt ☆ Arthur Robins

All priced at £3.99

Seriously Silly books are available from all good bookshops,
or can be ordered direct from the publisher:
Orchard Books, PO BOX 29, Douglas IM99 1BQ
Credit card orders please telephone 01624 836000
or fax 01624 837033
or e-mail: bookshop@enterprise.net for details.

To order please quote title, author and ISBN
and your full name and address.
Cheques and postal orders should be
made payable to 'Bookpost plc'.
Postage and packing is FREE within the UK
(overseas customers should add £1.00 per book).

Prices and availability are subject to change.